MW00624281

Praise for Donna Ashworth

'Soul-nurturing permission to relax,
connect and be kinder to ourselves.'
Fearne Cotton

'A little corner of calm within life's storm – wonderful.'
Cat Deeley

'Like a warm hug. Donna's words
are comfort for the soul.'
Tamzin Outhwaite

'Donna's much-needed words will no doubt
empower and lift our young people today.'
Lisa Faulkner

'Donna is a true wordsmith.
Her writings never fail to move me.'
Nadia Sawalha

'Donna's wise and beautiful words help us reach
a place of peace and acceptance. I would love to
have read them many years ago.'
Lisa Snowdon

'Donna has a rare gift of being able to put
into words how we all feel. Her writing is like
a hug from a wise friend.'
Samia Longchambon

Wild Hope

Also by Donna Ashworth:

To the Women

The Right Words

I Wish I Knew

Life

Love

Loss

Wild Hope

DONNA ASHWORTH

mango
PUBLISHING GROUP

CORAL GABLES

For permission requests, please contact the publisher at:
Mango Publishing Group
2850 S Douglas Road, 2nd Floor
Coral Gables, FL 33134 USA
info@mango.bz

For special orders, quantity sales, course adoptions and corporate sales, please email the publisher at sales@mango.bz. For trade and wholesale sales, please contact Ingram Publisher Services at customer.service@ingramcontent.com or +1.800.509.4887.

Wild Hope: Healing Words to Find Light on Dark Days

Library of Congress Cataloging-in-Publication number: has been requested
ISBNs: (hc) 978-1-68481-452-7 (e) 978-1-68481-471-8
BISAC category code: POE023020POETRY / Subjects & Themes /
Love & Erotica

The moral rights of the author have been asserted.

I dedicate this book to those I have learned from
along the way. Thank you for taking time to share
your lessons with me, and to guide me when I wavered.
Because of you, I shall go on to do the same.
And where sharing exists, hope grows,
like wild flowers on wasteland.

AUTHOR'S NOTE

I chose hope as the theme for this book because,
quite simply, without hope there is nothing.

Hope floats, it rises, it grows wild in the most
deprived soil and it can be the very difference
between life and death.

We have all heard stories of humans enduring the
unthinkable and surviving – no, *thriving*. Listen to
what they say and you will find hope in every chapter.

Hope exists when nothing else can and it is
an invisible yet powerful force we can all harness
from day to day. I watch people with avid fascination.
I read their tales of endurance and struggle and
I consume the hope they readily drip from every word.
You will find all of that hard-won inspiration
on these pages, to remind you of what you already
know to be true . . . you simply must have hope. It is the
light. It is the key. It is the fuel. And when you cannot
find yours, you can happily borrow mine.

CONTENTS

HOPE FLOATS

Hope *floats*, as a fated ship is dragged to its demise on
the seabed. Hope *rises* when everything else is sinking.
Hope *flies* when there are no wings and hope *drives*,
without an engine. Hope does not need light or oxygen
to survive. It grows best in the dark, truth be told.
Hope is the 1 per cent that rallies against statistics.
The one they cannot *explain*. Hope is against the odds,
in spite of fact and solely made of *will*. Hope is the space
between faith and spirit. Hope is the belief that things
can get better, that the sun will warm again, that the
end need not be that. Hope lives in the mud, in the mire,
in the barren wasteland of emptiness. It is like
magic, this hope. And the best thing of all? It's free;
you just have to call it near. Hope floats, my friends,
cling on to it when you are just too tired to swim.

AND ON WE GO

There is much power
in the phrase
and on we go

we break and rebuild
knowing we will break again
we lose but still love though
we know the pain won't end

we struggle along alone
yet we stop along the way
to help another stand
to see a brighter day

no matter what we have faced
how hard we have smashed
against the rocks of life

we wash up
we shed tears
we wail to the skies
we let go
we rest
we brush down
we shake off

and on we go . . .

DON'T LOSE HOPE

Put hope in a safe place. Not a *super-safe* place; the place we cleverly stash things in, never to be seen again. Just a safe, everyday place. Like beside your car keys. Put hope beside your car keys, and each time you leave the house, you'll see hope glistening there and you won't forget to take it with you. And if you're careful with hope, you'll never lose it again. You'll never experience that numb, hapless cloud that descends upon your life with its soul-sucking, vacuous apathy. Without your car keys, you're going nowhere. It's the same with hope. Hope is the engine, the steering wheel, the power in your life. Keep it safe. Don't lose hope. Keep it with your keys. You need it more than you may know.

SHADOWS

We have all awoken
sharply startled in the night
suddenly fearful
of the brooding shadow
in the corner of our room

hearts beating in our ears
we scramble for the light
only to be greeted
by a pile of clothes on a chair

life is like that

shine light into the dark corners
of your mind

take a good look
at the scary parts
you are afraid to enter into
they are quite different
once that light is on them
they cannot hold any power over you
in the burning glare of your shine

light them up my friends
light up the shadows
and scare them away
for good.

JOY CHOSE YOU

Joy does not arrive with a fanfare
on a red carpet strewn
with the flowers of a perfect life

joy sneaks in
as you pour a cup of coffee
watching the sun
hit your favourite tree
just right

and you usher joy away
because you are not ready for her
your house is not as it should be
for such a distinguished guest

but joy, you see
cares nothing for your messy home
or your bank balance
or your waistline

joy is *supposed* to slither through
the cracks of your imperfect life
that's how joy *works*

you cannot truly invite her
you can only be ready
when she appears
and hug her with meaning
because in this very moment
joy chose you.

RISK

Believing tomorrow
to be a guarantee
is the biggest mistake we make

not seizing every day
like the gift that it is
is the biggest risk we take

do what makes you happy
love your loved ones *fiercely*

speak up
say the words
do the *stuff*
ride the waves
head down through the storms
accept the dark
the light will follow

it's all part of it
it's life
it's meant to feel good
it's meant to feel hard
just feel it *all*

believing tomorrow
to be a guarantee
is the biggest mistake we make

not seizing every day
like the gift that it is
is the biggest risk we take.

TOO MANY SUNDAYS

Too many Sundays have been darkened by the dreaded presence of Monday, looming in like a storm cloud of fear, anxiety and gut-wrenching stress. Sunday is your gift, your day to recharge, your freedom. Be protective of that time. Monday has its space enough; do not let it overstep its mark. Make your plans, prepare, then push Monday back into its box and let Sunday shine forth like the jewel it is. You deserve this day of soul rest. Life is not a chore to be dealt with; it's to be lived, my friend. You're here to *live*. And Sunday is a day, gifted to us, for doing whatever your little heart desires.

REASON SEASON

Where are the books
on friendship break-ups?

pray, where are the self-help manuals
to pull you through that confusion
that *heartache*?

where are the songs
the poems
the words to help heal?

because if you have ever been there
you know
the pain of a lost connection

the torture of not knowing
where it went awry
the frustration of not being able
to fight for the love lost

where are the books
on friendship break-ups?

reason, season, lifetime
they say

but sometimes
the *reason* may not become known
and the *season*
is forever committed
to fond remembrance
for a *lifetime*.

UNLEASH

Don't be afraid to be alone until you find those people who can handle the whole of you – not just handle (you are not a trophy), but *relish*. Life is too precious to waste it being a slither, a slip, a 2D version of yourself. Make some time to accept all that you are – the messy, the raw, the loud and the joyous – and then go out there and take up some space without apologising for the realness you leave in your wake. Unleash, my friend, *unleash*. Life is only half-lived until you show up proud and true. Just you, being *you*, as only *you* can do.

LISTEN FOR ME

Listen for me in the music
in the songs we held so dear
I'll find a way to play them
so you will feel me near

each verse will lift your spirits
embrace your weary soul
each word my soul is sending
to help you feel more whole

listen for me in the music
and nature's music too
the birds will sing my message
they'll chorus my love for you

the wind will play the trees
as you are walking by
if you listen very closely
my heart's in every sigh

listen for me my love
I'll find a million ways
to whisper in your ear
that I'm not so far away.

A HANDFUL OF YEARS

There will come a day
when you will glance
at your child
and be met by an adult

and it will wipe the very floor
from under your feet
when you realise
in that moment
that you were only ever minding them
until they fly away

because back then
when you were so consumed
with the daily grind of parenting
you felt like this was *forever*

yet we know
nothing truly is *forever*

just a handful of years
you will know them as a child
and if you are blessed
many more
you will know them as an adult

drink them in
if you can
drink them in.

SURROUNDED BY TREASURE

Beautiful people are not always loved
rich folks get sad
for no reason
everyone goes through their share of the joys
and the pain
we all see every season

fabulous houses still let the rain in
designer bags
don't weather better
shiny new cars get to B just the same
you'll be warm
in an old or new sweater

bodies with six-packs ache and fall sick
gold watches
won't turn the time back
a house is a house till it's filled up with love
then a home
is what comes out of that

love what you have and you'll have what you love
it's the way to a life
full of pleasure
be kind to your life and your life will be kind
look around
you're surrounded by treasure.

Your battle to fit in was brave, but I hope you see that accepting you were never supposed to is much braver.

HELP SOMEONE ELSE

On those days when you are *stuck*, when you cannot see yourself for who you are, and you've no motivation to move, help someone else. Seek out someone to assist, with anything, as basic or as bold as you like. And as you are doing this *helping*, something wonderful occurs: your brain shifts from inward to *outward*, your heart shifts from apathy to *empathy*, your soul shifts from stuck to *doing something worthy*. Before you know it, you are so busy absorbing yourself in someone else's problem, being *useful*, that you may find your monkey brain has been silenced and your true brain, your *real* mind, has started to move forward again, all of its own accord. On the days when you can't help yourself, help someone else.

FORGOTTEN GRAVY

I love imperfectly mismatched rooms
homemade decorations
and trinkets
that tell stories of the past

I treasure impromptu gatherings
with food rustled up from nowhere
it's always just *enough*

I see the beauty in gifts handed over
with words of *oh it's nothin*g
for that simply means the giver
cannot begin to convey
how they really feel about you

I value both the quiet moments
when the lights twinkle privately
and the raucous occasions
when laughter fills the room

and I can't get enough of burnt carrots
forgotten gravy
and failed attempts at dessert

because that's where the love lives
in the imperfect
in the messy
in the real

love lives in the forgotten gravy
look for it.

NOW YOU DO

You don't have to defend the old you
you didn't know then
now you *do*
you did what you could
with what you had
at the time

and as with all things in life
you evolved
you've grown

if you find yourself
trying in vain
to defend the *old* you
to argue on her behalf
please stop
you don't have to do that

she was someone
you parted ways with
gracefully
but after much suffering

if anyone in your life
cannot do the same
that's their issue

*it's their job to catch up
not your job to go back*

you don't have to defend the old you
you didn't know then
now you do.

I hope you know that this beautifully messy life you are living will continue to create great love, even after you leave.

JUST A DAY

No, today probably won't be a great day, but it absolutely won't be a bad day either. Today will simply be a day. Twenty-four hours of a little bit of everything. Some moments will be hard, some will be joyous, some will be peaceful and some will be draining. And you, you will handle it all, because that's what you *do*. Don't put pressure on yourself to have any kind of a day, my friend. Life throws enough at you. Instead, just remind yourself that whatever happens, you are ready. And most importantly, you have your own back. It's just a day. Another day of life in all its messy everything-ness. **Lucky us.**

THE MOON AND I

I have always loved the moon
but now
she and I are locked
in an eternal pact of hope

I ask her how you are
and she lets me know
you're peaceful
blissful
reminding me
you still exist within my own bones
and that she's simply reflecting that back
so I can see it more clearly

I ask her not to stop
never to stop

I have always loved the moon
but now she holds me in the night
when I need to see your face
I look at hers instead
and she shows me *you*, my love
she reflects you right back

and I ask her not to stop
never to stop

I always loved the moon
but now
she and I are locked
in an eternal pact of hope
an eternal *remembering*

of you.

IN THE PHOTO

It's easy to shy away from photographs because you're so busy, so exhausted, not feeling your best. It's easy to be the *taker* and never let yourself be in, when holidays make you feel exposed or *less than*. But one day, your loved ones will search for those memories to bolster their own. Those pictures, no matter how you look, are set to become absolutely **precious**. And no one, not one of them, will care how *together* you appear. They will care, very much, that it is *you*. And all of your *you-ness* will be the exact gift they very much need in that moment. Be in the photo, my friends. *They are not for you.*

YOU DON'T MEET ANYONE
BY ACCIDENT

You don't meet anyone in this life
by accident

some are sent to teach you
what love *is*
some are sent to teach you
what love most certainly *isn't*

some are sent to support you
without falter
and those you must hold
very dear indeed

others are sent to challenge
your self-worth
never let them win

some people are taken
far too soon
and the lesson there
is to live life fully
here and now
and love deeply
with every moment you have

you don't meet anyone in this life
by accident
each person brings with them
a *joy*
a *love*
or a *lesson*
pay attention.

WITHOUT YOU

How do I live without you?
oh, my love, I do not

you are with me from the moment
I open my eyes
until they close
and even after that
on the plane of dreams
where souls and mortals meet
you are with me still

I've not begun to live without you
perhaps I never will
the truth of the matter is
you are always with me still

you walked such a blazing pathway
when your feet were on this earth
that your imprint lingers on
and I place my own feet
in your steps
one by one

how do I live without you?
It's really very simple
I do not

I have yet to live without you
perhaps I never will
perhaps the key to grief is
you are always with me still.

THE AFTER-PARTY PEOPLE

Anyone can fill a room full of glittering people.
Announce a party, send out invitations, bring food,
wine, music and the promise of fun, they will come.
But it is the after-party people you must treasure
in this life. The ones who stay to help clear away.
The ones who see you are exhausted from the
organising, and know you will need them then.
The ones who call the day before and say, *What can
I help you with?*, despite being already overwhelmed
in their own lives. The people who will show up for
your house move, for your worst days, for your *broken*.
The people who stay when the show is over, the curtain
has fallen heavily to the stage floor and the make-up
is off. It is wonderful to be surrounded by fun-filled
faces sometimes, but you only need one face, one little
loving face, full of care and friendship, to thrive.

WHEN MY TIME COMES

I pray that when my time comes
no one waxes lyrical
about the quality of my skin
for my age

I pray that no one
compliments my corpse
on its great condition

I want everyone
to remember
me
the way I showed my face
to the sun
without care for lines
and how I wore my body out
every minute
of every day
in the most beautiful
and love-filled ways

I was not here to preserve
I came to *live*
and my body
will tell that story
the story of my soul *well*

when my time comes.

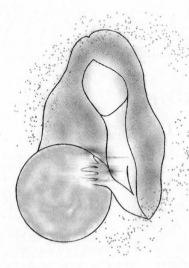

YOU

If every single person who has liked you in your lifetime were to light up on a map, it would create the most glitteringly beautiful network you could imagine. Throw in the strangers you've been kind to, the people you've made laugh, or inspired along the way, and that star-bright web of **you** would be an impressive sight to behold. You're so much more than you think you are.

You have done so much more than you realise. You're trailing a bright pathway that you don't even know about. What a thing. *What a thing indeed.*

DEAR DAUGHTER

I hope with all my heart
that I showed you the real *me*
that I didn't pretend I had it all together
or that life was not hard

I hope I gave you the belief of *you* in your core
that I loved you enough, albeit messily
to code a blueprint for life
to show you what love should *look like*

I hope I let you see me break
so you could understand it's not an ending
rather a *step*
and it's vital

Dear daughter
I could not possibly have gotten everything right
and perhaps that's the best thing I have given you
the knowledge that no one gets it right
we are not here to be *perfect*
we are here to grow stronger
and more bright
with every generation

grow brighter my love
brighter than me
as it very much should be
and when I can no longer be here, *remember*
my cells live within you
you cannot ever lose me, not really

we are a deal, a two-for-one
I won't ever be too far.

I hope you walk the quickest path to peace;
to strive for *less* in a world that
wants so much *more*.

TO MY BOY

The bond a mother has with her son
is like a beautiful black hole
of utter love and adoration
it is all-consuming
never-ending and mightier than us

women know one another by intuition and instinct
you see
we are of the *same*
but when a woman creates a boy
something else quite magical happens
I hope I showed you that power
that *force*

I hope I taught you what it is to respect a woman
to respect *all* humans
and to never lose yourself in the process

I pray you see how strong you are
by allowing yourself to be soft
that's the *key*

and most of all
I hope you check your heart
when you cannot pick up the phone to me
check the little chasms of your heart, my love
that's where I stored the things you need
the *love* you need

my boy
my beautiful *beautiful* boy
you had me at first sight
and you have me forevermore.

WITHOUT HOPE

Without hope, grief will surely steal your life. Without believing you will see them again, that they still exist around you in energy, that their love is fuelling yours, grief will make a wasteland of your world. Do not let something born of such beauty, of such joy, become your downfall. It was supposed to be your purpose, the fire in your belly, the reason you go on. Hope is the space between having them here and knowing they are still with you. It is an invisible blanket but, oh, it will warm you at night. Let it warm you, my friends.

Let the love, and the hope, warm you.

THE WITCH WOUND

They call it the witch wound
we were *punished,* you see
broken, slain
for shining too brightly

so we learned to hide that spark
we learned to play it down
play dumb, play *dead*

and we were taught to fear
the light within us
lest it herald our downfall

but not anymore

you are not a witch, my friend
you are quite simply
or *complicatedly*
a woman

and your magic is not something
you can choose, or lose
it always is
and always has
lived within you

and you need no longer hide it

they call it the witch wound
but the time to heal is here
now
let that magic out.

SPRING

I have always believed spring to be *the* harbinger of hope, the launch pad to lighter days, the gateway to life. Spring soothes our winter-worn souls with anticipation, and its promise of *more*. It gently shakes our hibernating toes and whispers, *wake now, your wintering days are done.* And so, with each eager sunrise, we emerge, we reignite, we re-energise. And as with the nature around us, we begin to rise and renew. Come on in, spring, we have much longed for your light, for your joy, for your *new*. We are slowly rousing from slumber, welcome back.

SUMMER

Summertime, when the living is easy.
When life is at its bountiful peak and days are
so deliciously long, there is no end to the promise
they hold. Summer is the time to be alive, to make hay
while the sun shines and to fill your energy stores with
memories of joy, which will fill the otherwise empty
hearths of your heart with fire, all winter long. Do not
let worries or fears stop you from embracing the sun,
the *joy*, you so deserve, my friends. You are gifted
many summers in your life, but never quite enough.
You deserve to *live* them. To feel them. Summertime,
when the living is easy, so live *easy*.

AUTUMN

Most rejoice at the sight of spring, but I have
always loved autumn. Rich, righteous colours, a
shedding of weight and submission to a force larger
than you. The revelation of one's true self. Bare and
unafraid. Warmed and dressed not by folly, but by
innate wisdom. And the *knowing*, that this is as it
must be and *everything will pass*. Autumn does not
shudder at the thought of winter ahead; it peacefully
basks in the last of the sun, counting every moment
as a blessing and a vital part of the journey. It lets
its leaves fall to the ground to nurture the new,
like droplets of nourishing gold, and finds peace
where no peace existed before. I've always loved
autumn. It's the letting go, you see. Let it *go*.

WINTERING

You may think yourself lazy, or flawed. Yet your body
is made of almost exactly the same elements as the stars.
Your bone composition matches perfectly the coral
in the seas, and you, my friend, are ruled by the moon
and the sun, the tides and the planets. Whether you
like it or not. So, no, you are not *lazy*, you are not *late*.
Nature is simply pulling you to slow, like the life, flora
and fauna around you. It is not your moment to rise.
Look around you. It is winter. You are *wintering*.
And you are right on time.

CATCH THE COMPLIMENTS

I have seen a hundred compliments
launched lovingly in your direction
that you swatted away like flies in summer

and I have seen too
a handful of hurtful words
fired at your fortifications
which you immediately allowed through
picked up with both hands
made a home for in your heart
and kept for all time

then on days when your heart is sore
you reach for those dark words that hurt
and press them till they hurt more

and the compliments?
they floated away on the breeze
never to be seen again

my friend, I wish, from this day on
that you begin to catch those compliments
shine them to display on a shelf, in full view
and chase those harmful words from your door
never to be seen again

and so, to begin your collection
you are warm, unique, loving and kind
the world is so much better with you in it

I hope this launches a **hundred more**.

WHEN I'M NO LONGER HERE

When I'm no longer here
say my name to call me near
I will calm your disarray
move mountains from your way
I will dry your falling tears
whisper comfort in your ear
when I'm no longer here
say my name to call me near

when I'm a glowing star
do not think of me as far
I am with your inner child
hoping you'll embrace your wild
seeking joy in every day
finding jewels of light in grey
when I'm a glowing star
do not think of me as far

when I'm no longer here
let me rid your heart of fear
put it down upon the floor
I'll take it from your door
give me then your worry too
let me carry it for you
when I'm no longer here
let me rid your heart of fear.

THE RISE OF THE ELDERS

Bring back the rise
of the *Elders*

the wise
the revered

the fabulously *aged*
and *learned*

society is amiss
of this order right now

we dismiss the old
ignore them
when we should be placing them
atop bedazzled pedestals
drinking in their every word

for the treasure maps of this life
live within their stories

bring back the rise
of the *Elders*

let's flip the perspective again
and see ageing as the *prize*
the achievement
the RISE
that it is.

LOVE LANGUAGE

That thing you do
tagging friends in posts
you *know*
will land like rain on thirsty soil

the texts you send
just to show
they're nestled amongst your thoughts
and in your soul vision

the remedies you share
with such hope
of *healing*

the videos you save
knowing they will reach inside their very heart
and draw their lips into a smile
much-needed

that
all of that
is a love language

and it's absolutely beautiful.

I HOPE

As you sleep so soundly
I dream of who you'll be
how you'll make this world your own
and if I'll live to see

I wonder of your life
and the things you'll choose to do
I hope a love will find you
like the love I have for you

I think of how you'll look
if you'll let your hair stay wild
or if the world will smooth the edges
of my vibrant whirlwind child

I pray you'll see your beauty
and be grateful for your heart
I will your soul to stay intact
and make this life your art

I hope you'll guard your kindness
and that infectious beaming smile
I know you'll be their sunshine
you've been mine for such a while

I can't make life accept you
or clear your path of pain
all I can do is love you
and hope you'll do the same.

THE UNINVITED FRIEND

I have an uninvited friend
she came to my door last night
again
and I almost pretended to be out
but it was too late
she saw me peering through the blinds
and she can sense my energy anyway

I let my friend in
and she wrapped her arms around me
uninvited
we stayed there like that
quietly
just some sobbing
some sighing
and a little silent crying

without saying a single word
my friend gave me three things
she gave me a hug
my favourite ice cream
and best of all
she gave me back my hope

I had lost it again you see
outside somewhere
and she found it like she always does

and brought it back to me
uninvited
I hope you have an uninvited friend like mine
I can't imagine life without one.

When it's all falling apart, when the only thing you have left is *hope*, you have all you need to go on.

RIGHT NOW

What if you get to the end of your life and you suddenly make the connection, that you were supposed to enjoy it? That you were supposed to let go and live, make stories to pass on, because material possessions don't bring half as much joy as the memories of love that you leave? What if you realise, too late, that your cellulite and tummy rolls were adorable actually and should never, ever, have been enough to stop you having fun? What if your last thoughts were regrets for not enjoying this ride, and giving it all that you had? What if you stopped that from happening, right here, right now? What if . . .?

A DAY IS NOT LOST

A day is not lost
if you failed to tick off a list
or a diet was broken

a day is only lost
if you forgot
to say something kind
to yourself
or another

if you forgot
to pause
to search
for a tiny spark of beauty
amongst the drudgery
glimmering like gold
in the mud

a day is only lost
if you forgot
that life
even in the worst of times
is still a *gift*
a gift you so very much deserve
to *live* through

and not just **survive**.

IT'S YOU OR IT

There is a point at which *that thing*
will consume you
the thing you have allowed
to live rent-free inside your head for so long

you spar back and forth
some days *the thing* will win
dimming your light a little
and other days you will be the victor
as you cram its invisible bulk
into a box within your brain

but this war cannot trundle on unwon
at some point that thing
will consume you, my friend
if you let it

it is time *high time* to call it out
face it squarely in the eye
delve into its mass to see
exactly what it is made of
strip it all back
through the chaos
the pain and the sorrow
because underneath it all
whatever that thing may be
exists a lack of love

and whilst you cannot change the past
you can ensure a better future

there is a point at which that *thing*
will consume you
it's you or *it*
choose **you**.

There is much hope to be found buried in mud; after all, that's where the most beautiful flowers thrive best.

TOO MUCH

Life does not just feel like too much sometimes, it **is**. We were built to love, to nurture, to survive. Everything else is extra. And it can be a beautiful bonus, the extra, as long as you do not fall into the trap of believing it all matters. What matters is how you live whilst you are here, how you respect this planet and those on it, how you love those gifted into your life and how you leave, having done as much of all of that as possible. Life does not just feel like too much sometimes, it *is* too much. Choose your list of priorities wisely.

TIME CAN'T ERASE YOUR BEAUTY

Ageing looks good
on anyone who *believes* that it does

it's an inner light kind of deal

it shines through skin, bone
muscle and sinew
bathing everything you see
in a luminous glow of peace
acceptance
and utter **loveliness**

It's some sort of chemical reaction
when self-love (at last)
meets Mother Nature
then wisdom and hindsight
all join together too
and cast their magic
until what you see is a woman
who has evolved, grown
learned and risen
many many times

and it's a beautiful sight to behold

time can't erase your beauty, my friend
only negativity can do that.

RIGHT AT THE TOP

It bothers me when people say mental health
is just as important as physical health, because
no, it is not. It's *more* important. Your brain,
your mind, your computer, runs the entire show.
Quite literally nothing, nothing, in your body works
without your mind. If it is not constantly maintained,
understood and managed, it will bring everything
else to its knees. Everything. I'm pleased the
world is finally waking up to the importance
of mental health, but let's prioritise it properly,
finally. Right at the top. Where it belongs.

MEMORY

I promise you this
as the years take their toll
my memory may fade
but never my soul

I may not seem the same
to the unknowing eye
I might mix my words
and cause you to cry

names may elude me
and places confuse
time may escape me
and days I may lose

but your little face
with its cheeks ever bright
will live in my dreams
in the still of the night

your spirit so brave
is still etched in my heart
so never forget
how I loved from the start

I promise you this
as the years change my brain
I'll remember the *love*
that will always remain.

THROUGH THE WRINGER

My granny used to say, *you've been through the wringer*.
And I felt those words deeply. Because life is a wringer.
We squeeze ourselves dry, giving, *giving*, our whole
lives long. Digging *deeper*. Going *further*. Being *more*.
And just when we think we are dry, we are *out*, we find
another drop of sacred self to save someone in need.
But here's the thing, my friends . . . the wringer must not
be final, it's supposed to be a fluid exercise; we soak,
we are wrung dry, we do it all again. So don't forget
to soak. That's the vital element in this journey,
the *soak*. Keep soaking.

TIME CANNOT

Money can return
time *cannot*

make your memories now
whilst the opportunities appear

you will never regret
the adventures you took
my friends

you may
however
forever be saddened
by those you let pass by

and when days darken
as they surely will
those memories you made
they will *warm* you

fuel you

drive you on

to do more *living*

*money can return
time cannot.*

I LOOKED BACK

I looked back
and saw beaches
sunsets
glasses clinking together
teeth shining in the light

I looked back
and saw tables filled with food
bread broken in togetherness
hearts sharing tears
and so much laughter

I looked back
and saw risks taken
hands squeezed
lessons learned
love flourishing

I looked back
and saw
tough times faced
problems shared
and triumphs
hard-won

I looked back
and didn't see
my failures
my flaws
or my
not being enough-ness

I didn't see
wrinkles
cellulite
or numbers on scales

I *didn't* see
cars
possessions
or money made

I looked back
and saw
a life
lived to the full

and full includes
the sadness
the loss
the *living*

look back sometimes
my friends
if you can

it will remind you
what is important
or perhaps
more *importantly*

what is not.

Care not for fact when I am gone from sight;
cling to the blissful hope that love is enough
to bring us together again.

ALL MY HEART

We are not, and never will be *perfect*. Thank goodness.
But when I met you, and let you inside my walls, little
pieces of me I had forgotten about came back. As though
they recognised you before I did. As though they saw a
safe place to breathe, at last. And little by little, I started
to feel more whole. It's not that you completed me, it's
that you loved me enough that I could complete myself.
So when I say I love you with *all* my heart, I mean it.
Because it is *all*, again. And I think – no, I *know*,
that you *safed* it back to life.

WITH YOUR KNOWING

Let us not talk of regaining our youth
of appearing *unchanged*

let us talk instead
of how we have *weathered* this stormy ride
how we have *consumed* life
in all its splendour
the good, the bad
and each crazy step in-between

let us regale each other with scars
and survival stories
pass those treasures down
to all who may listen and thrive
as though the words breathe very life
into their air-quenched lungs

we are not here to be *still*
we are here to break beautifully
again and again
into shards of shimmering dust
to fall down beatifically
on the generations beneath

like a disco-ball rainstorm
of wisdom and learning
we must shine our light *wildly*

let us not talk of regaining our youth
when we have gained so much more with our years
light up the world, my friends
light up the world
with your *knowing*.

JUST WOMEN

It must have been a terrifying sight to behold
a group of witches gathered by firelight
chanting, conjuring spirits
creating spells
little wonder some were *afraid*

but I think it was just women
being *women*

coming together
as they very much must
to support one another
to share their battles
pull each other through the flames
they faced daily

sharing remedies
medicines
ways to heal

believing they were so much more than told
than *allowed*

it is little wonder that the power of this union
would appear like *magic*
to the unknowing eye

but I think it was just **women**
doing what we do
every day.

I'M ONE OF THOSE WOMEN

I'm one of those women who will tell you what I think of you, even though you may not like it. Because I will tell you that you are glorious, imperfectly perfect. For what could be more perfect than *real*? What could be better than your you-ness? I will tell you that your laugh is like music and your worries are important and valid. I will tell you that your thoughts are fascinating and so very worthy of airtime. That your jokes are a little burst of sunshine in my day. I will tell you that you are not your mistakes and you're never unlovable. I will tell you all of this and you may not like it, because you have not yet begun to enjoy the unashamed validation of someone who just adores you for the right reasons. But you should, and you will. So, if you don't like women who tell you exactly what they think, stay away from me, my friend, because I won't ever stop.

YOU CAN'T FIX THEM

You can't fix them
but you can tell them
how the cracks in their armour
let the light shine through
and how beautiful that is

you can't bring them back
but you can take the love
they selflessly showed you
and give it to the world
in their honour

you can't heal them
but you can heal yourself
and show them *how*
the pain will lose its bite
if you smother it in light

you can't make them happy
but you can make them *smile*
and you can show up
sit with them
and let them know
they are accepted
no matter what

sometimes
that is all we need.

YOU HAVE BEEN SERVED

If you are lucky enough to wake one day
and feel the pull of something *bigger*
something almost magical
inviting you to follow
go, my friend, *go*

you have been *served* by Mother Nature

she comes for us all
when the time is right
to show us a better
more *peaceful* way to be
a way in which we can actually enjoy
this life of ours
build ourselves *space* to flourish
space to breed joy

no more existing, she will say
time to be alive
no more surviving, she will add
time to thrive

she waits until you are truly done
berating and twisting
into a million punishing shapes to please

she waits until you sit down one day
exhausted again
and wish for a better way

if you are lucky enough to feel that powerful hand
reach in and pull you up, go, my friend

your moment has arrived and you won't look back.

A beautiful face is any face, worn
by a soul full of light, love and hope.
No mirror will show you that.

HEAVEN

What if we do go to heaven? What if heaven is as wondrous as they say, and we exist in light and peace, surrounded by those we lost? And what if we do look down from our blissful abode and see the ones we left behind, shutting out light and cancelling joy, to honour our absence? My friend, please do not let life die with them. Because I'm sure, beyond sure in fact, that it would be the last thing they'd want. We must, we *must*, honour their *life*, by living ours, with their love as the motivation. And we can honour our grief too, that's the way. *That's the way.* Their spirit did not die, only their body. Do not let your spirit go with them. Not yet. *Not yet.*

TO THE WIND

Count the days spent *living*
put them in a pile
add the loving moments
where you lingered for a while

count the sun-drenched beaches
the waves that cleansed your heart
coupled with the risks you took
that beckoned life to start

take the joyful memories
the ones that grew your soul
the music that entranced your mind
the words that made you whole

the taste of salty kisses
wiping tears and fears away
the warmth of little bodies
before they flew away

picture all the faces
you loved throughout the years
take a mental screenshot
they are yours to carry near

put all these things together
in a file marked
what I know
take all other memories
to the wind
and
let them go . . .

YOU *ARE* NATURE

There is a reason why walking amongst nature is most people's best advice when depression strikes. Because walking in nature is a return to *home*. You are not a lover of nature or in need of some nature; you *are* nature. You are as much nature as the trees in your garden and the bees on your picnic. You were designed to live your days out in the wild with your fellow creatures and plants, but progress, *humanity*, had different plans for us all. And so we exist day-to-day, in our homes, but never *home*. The quickest route back to self, to inner peace, is bare feet on grass, arms around trees, head in the clouds and heart in a forest. Put your weary body in water, whenever you can. Smell every flower you see and crumble dirt between your tired-of-typing fingers. You *are* nature, so go home once in a while. It will bring you so much you didn't even know you were missing.

I CANNOT BE REACHED

The power in the *knowing*
that I'm no longer available
for the drama
or the shallow

that I'm no longer a place
on a map
for the wrong
to seek out
and *make a home in*

the joy in the *realising*
that I cannot be reached
without love as a token
without respect as a ticket

unless your purpose
is kind and clear
my walls are high
you won't get near

the peace in the *receiving*
this gift
is by far the best

I have ever unwrapped.

TEN FEET TALL

Some say that she's been fading
as the years are passing by
a shadow of her former self
they talk and wonder why

her clothes no longer chic
her hair pulled back and greying
the way she lets her wrinkles show
to some, is most dismaying

but what they do not see
is the light she's found within
I don't know how they miss it
or how they think it dim

to me she glows with wisdom
she radiates such peace
and as she passes, I can hear
the truth she'd surely preach

she's let some things slip by
there is truth in that for sure
but her youth is still the last thing
she would pick up from the floor

for she found herself one day
the woman trapped inside
and now she pays no heed
to how society divides

she is focused on the light
on the meaning of it all
and though she shrinks in size
to me she's ten feet tall.

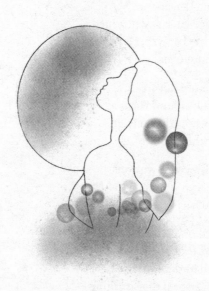

THEY HAVE US

I thought about the moon last night, how she has no light source of her own. How what we see in the midnight sky is simply a majestic rock, reflecting the light of the sun back to us to ensure we are never without guidance, never without *hope*. Then I considered how, without the moon, our planet would tilt wildly, experiencing extreme weather and uninhabitable conditions, as each side of our earth faced *too much* light, or *too little*. And I guess what I am trying to say is, this galaxy, our planet, is a *magical*, *wondrous* thing. And we are all held in place by it. We are not alone, and we are never without support. Don't fear the long nights, my friend, look to the skies for reassurance, that light always comes back. The sun and the moon, they *have* us. And they work together, diligently, to ensure we go on. So *go on*.

WASTING TIME

Perhaps we could redefine
our idea of *time*

I don't believe you can *waste* time
by resting
talking to a friend
walking in nature
or reading a book

you can't waste time by connecting
letting souls talk
allowing inner children out to play
or making stories to pass down

you can't waste time by helping
or doing anything at all
that feeds your soul
and energises your weary bones

that's exactly what time is for
in fact
everything else
is just a tick on a list

just a tick
on a never-ending list.

WRITE ME DOWN

If one day I don't remember
do not feel *helpless*
you have much work to do

you must remember me enough for two
write me down

place the things that make me *me*
in a beautiful box
my treasured photos
my joyous memories

build my essence whole again
with pictures, words, music, recipes
things that sparked my spirit

if one day I begin to fade, my love
do not feel *hopeless*
put yourself straight to this pursuit

I was very much here
so very much alive
you know that better than anyone

you know me enough for the world
so tell the world who I am
because if I have forgotten *me*
it is vital that *you* don't

remember me, my love
remember all of me
enough for two

and then I won't be gone.

YOU ARE POETRY

Poetry flows through your fingers
each time you send a morning text
a beacon of hope to arrive just in time
as anxiety is pulling in the driveway

poetry breathes through your patience
as you scare away the angry words
circling ahead like hungry birds
but you choose kinder ones instead
words to help the heal

poetry lives in you, my friend
every time you share an ugly truth
that reaches in and pulls someone up
out of the mire, with its *knowing*
that caring, proverbial, hand to stand

ask anyone who loves you
they will tell you of a thing you said
that brought in light and chased the dread
that net you cast to catch them as they fell

you may not even see it
but you do love poetry
you are poetry
you speak it every day.

AWAKENING

The older I get, the more I realise that all this talk
of women having gone mad is actually just women
waking up one day, smelling the coffee and feeling
furious. Furious that they twisted themselves like
a pretzel all these years trying to conform to what
others wanted them to be. Furious that they didn't
say *no* more, or – more to the point – that they
didn't say *hell no* more. Furious that they didn't
say *yes* more, that they didn't feel they could put
themselves first. Furious that their feelings, their
emotions and their desires were branded as hormonal
all these years, as a lame excuse to fob them off and
not face up to bad behaviour. And no, this is not
just the menopause. This is called awakening. The
older I get the more I realise that women are not going
mad. In fact, they are becoming very sane indeed.

MOTHER NATURE'S HAND

I think stretchmarks, wrinkles, freckles and moles are
by Mother Nature's paintbrush. I think love-handles,
thigh-dimples and birthmarks are also by her fair hand.
I think *flaws* and *imperfections* are the most interesting
part of anyone's body. That crooked tooth, which squeezes
my heart each time her smile flashes. That dimple. The
way her face swallows her eyes when she laughs, so she
can laugh harder and let go of all care. The line that forms
between her eyebrows when her thoughts are hard. I think
everyone, *everyone*, is a work of art, actually. Like a
magic picture. You just have to step back and really *see*.

LET THEM

Let them argue
let them fight
let them believe
they are right

let them gossip
let them rage
let them build
themselves a cage

let them judge
let them talk
let them walk
the way they walk

let them laugh
behind your back
they cannot push you
from your track

let them steal
each other's joy
let them silence
virtue's voice

let them wrestle
for the throne
let them pick flesh
from their bones

but of all
you let them do
do not let them
alter you

keep your focus
on the sky
and all the beauty
you pass by

stay within
your well-built walls
and answer only
worthy calls

let them lie
if they must
it's yourself
you need to trust.

I hope you find at least one right person
who will like you in a way that a
hundred wrong people could not.

TODAY, I HOPE

I hope you see the beauty in the bland today
I hope you laugh until those tears just flow
I hope you let your soul be as it must today
I hope you'll finally learn to let it go

I hope the winds of change will blow your way today
I hope your heart is beating strong and true
I hope you'll let the warmth inside your world today
I hope you'll find some kindness there for you

I hope you like the way your story goes today
I hope you see the hero there is you
I hope you'll write the chapter you deserve today
I hope the happy ending will come true

I hope you know the impact that you have today
I hope you see your light for what it is
I hope you do not pick yourself apart today
I hope you know this life is yours to live

I hope you feel the sun upon your face today
I hope you'll share a moment with a love
I hope you find some comfort in this place today
I hope you also take some comfort from above.

YOU'RE NOT FOR EVERYONE

You're not for everyone
but you are most definitely
for *someone*

and when you find yourself caught
in the trap of *people-pleasing*
remind yourself quickly
that you are *people* too

and further refresh your memory
by recalling
that pleasing everyone
is not possible

it cannot be done
just like the sun cannot shine
on all faces at once

but when it does
when you *are* for someone
it is more than enough

you're not for everyone
my love
but it's the *someones*
who matter most
the *someones*
who will breathe you new life
when your lungs forget how

love your *someones*
love them fiercely.

CHECK YOUR VIBES

Do not dull your light
to match another's

do not dim your frequency
to fit a muted room

do not lower your vibration
for fear of standing out

and do not ever
EVER
try to lower someone else's

do not allow shouting voices
to drown your instinct

and do not silence your instinct
when she is screaming at you to hear

vibes are not *woo-woo*, my friends
they are the energy that runs
this mystical rock we inhabit

and they control everything

**check your vibes
never dim**

it's the new *chin up*.

DRIVE YOUR ANXIETY

The thing about anxiety is that it feeds on itself. The more anxious you are, the more anxious you get. The fear of that heightening is so very real, it escalates the growth even further. Until you are completely and utterly overwhelmed. No longer in charge of your vehicle. The anxiety is driving now. And the only thing you can do, to stop the take-over, is to remove the food source. To sit down, breathe in, breathe out, again, AGAIN. Remind the body that *you* are the master. *You* belong in the driver's seat. Remind your body that you have the power over your lungs, your life-givers. They move to *your* command. And anxiety is just an unwanted guest that you can relegate to the backseat once more, where it belongs. Drive your anxiety – do not let it drive you.

REST HERE AWHILE

Rest here awhile
you have walked a rough road
and you scarce held
a comforting hand

you've known so much dark
and you wrestled that load
drop it here
because I understand

rest here awhile
you're no longer alone
and there's much pain
for you to unpack

you've faced stormy nights
and you've more up ahead
but I'm here now
I'll stand at your back

rest here awhile
there's no pressure to be
just a place where your heart
can crack open

let your scars be on show
I have scars of my own
we need not be ashamed
of our broken

rest here my friend
you are safe now at last
release all the fear
from your heart

breathe out all the way
let light warm your face
it is time for your healing
to start.

IN REST, THEY REMEMBER

Some people are slowly taken
to the other realm
not physically, but mentally
memory by memory
they are pulled from us
like a painstakingly slow house-move

boxes full of life
chapters, people, loves
all packed into a van
to await their arrival on the other side

and as these parts are removed
those left feel lonelier daily
as though their love is already leaving them

it is a painful departure, my friends
this much is sadly true

but I like to think of the person we knew
reaching the other side, *finally*
once more *whole*
and upon arrival they see their boxes
awaiting them so long
they open them up
the chapters, the memories, the loves
and reunite with them all again

I can feel that heartfelt joy
and it brings me joy too
they are not lost for long
though it may feel so
in rest
they remember it all.

HEART OUTSIDE

Being a parent is like wearing your heart outside
of your body. Then, after years spent nurturing,
growing, protecting, keeping alive, letting that heart
wander off on its own, into a world, we know, can do
such harm to it. And all we can hope for, is that our
heart calls home, updates us sometimes, with their
stories, their safety, their happiness, their troubles.
We can only wish that we will be asked to help mend
that heart when needed, a job we have long trained in.
Being a parent is like wearing your heart outside
of your body, and knowing that's exactly
where it's *supposed* to be.

MOTHER'S DAY

If Mother's Day is hard for you – and there are many reasons why it could be – remember, sweet one, how *loved* you are. How your very existence itself is a miracle of science, nature and luck. And how luck may wane but love never does. If you have a mother in heaven, bring her here today and celebrate the legacy she leaves behind daily. If you never knew a mother's love, be aware: you can *create* it. You can be the start of that love anew and spread it to everyone in your world – child, friend or stranger. *You* can do that. If Mother's Day is hard for you, find a way, my friend. A way to celebrate *creation*, to celebrate *nurture*, to celebrate the people in your life who have *loved* you. Many of us mother every day, in many ways, and not always with our children. Happy Mother's Day.

GIVEN TOO MUCH

I think you have given too much
I think, *too many*
have become *too used*
to your constant support
your enduring reliability
your unwavering care

and I think, it is time
beyond time, in fact
for you to review these boundary lines
which have become so very blurred

yes, I think, you have given too much

and now, I think, it is time
beyond time, in fact
for you to give *more*

to yourself

more to your dreams
more to your joy
more to your *being*

you have given too much
but you have time left still
to give even more

to the things you left behind

and, I think, you left yourself behind

go back for her.

Take those shattered pieces and create
the most beautiful mosaic you can imagine;
hope will be the glue.

A FEARLESS GIRL

I knew a fearless girl
who shook the whole damn world
with her muddy knees and hands
that defiant way she'd stand

she took everything they knew
scrunched it up and wrote anew
she cared nothing for false rules
she was wiser than these fools

and with every day she grew
stronger, brighter, pushing through
till her heart was stole away
by a boy who watched her play

he took pieces of her soul
every day he made a hole
chipped away, at all she'd got
till her spirit seemed to rot

and as time went marching on
they feared that girl they knew was gone
till one day, like lightning strike
she was woken in the night

as though touched by someone passed
she was wide awake at last
you know well what love looks like
you're confused, this isn't right

just like that, her spirit rose
she found her back, wrinkled her nose
and remembered who she was
felt the pang for all she'd lost

till this day, that fearless girl
now grown up, out in the world
is a dreamer and a Queen
helping others to feel seen

and she's thankful to that voice
who helped her make that choice
because the simple, basic truth
is that *you're* too much to lose.

MAN UP

The world can be tough
for a boy who's not rough
there's much pressure
to *man up* and fight

and the boys who shout loud
seem so very proud
to preach that this macho
is right

and since boys may not talk
in the way that they ought
it's a lonely old life
for the gentle

they hide their sweet thoughts
their tears can't be caught
lest they're branded
as too sentimental

but I wish those boys knew
that their heart will push through
there's no way to extinguish
that beauty

being tough's not a goal
letting love in your soul
should be more than
considered a duty

I will raise gentle boys
who can use their heart voice
I will praise every tear
and emotion

let the gentle boys rise
let the world have fresh eyes
let *man up* be no longer
a notion.

WOMEN KNOW

Women *know*
even when we don't know
we still just *know*
you know?

and that is hard to explain
to those who don't *know*

but we do, we just
quite *simply*
do

and the most sad thing
a woman can do
in this life, I think
is start to shut down
that *knowing*

that *intuition*

because it is a gift
from those fearless females
who passed before us
paving the way
with their bravery
their fire
their flame

so go on *knowing*
my friends

keep the knowing *flowing*

it is your **power**.

THREADS FROM HEAVEN

I see you look to the sky, as you think of your loved ones, and I believe there is much power in that act. For at least a million others are looking right now too. And that collective power, of loss, of **love**, is a wonderful thing to imagine. Imagine with me now, my friends . . . a million people with hearts radiating upwards, sending so much love. And a million souls radiating love right back in response. Invisible, magical threads of love, woven all across the planet, **threads from heaven**.

THE TREASURE BOX

When I was nine, they bought me a box
to keep all my treasures inside
it was shiny, pretty, dazzlingly new
with sweet etchings along every side

as time went along, the box became full
of things that I wanted to keep
a stub for a show, where we laughed till we cried
the bracelet we found on the beach

the box grew so full, stretched at the seams
the etchings were faded and worn
the hinges were fragile, eaten by rust
and the beautiful lining was torn

yet the treasures inside, were perfectly kept
and when opened the joy within gleamed
like a beautiful trip down memory lane
the life that I lived brightly beamed

alas now the box, was breaking apart
but it'd done what it came here to do
it had treasured a life within its sweet heart
and I hope that's what I'm doing too.

YOU ARE

Some say you are what you eat
but I think it's *deeper* than that
I think you are who you *love*
and *what* you love, matter of fact

some say you are what you do
and for some, perhaps that's right
but I think you are what you *laugh* at
and the thoughts you have deep in the night

I think you are all the *words*
that pierced their way into your soul
the *songs* that you played on repeat
the *people* who make you feel whole

you're every sweet *gesture* you've made
and every *tear* you've ever shed
you are all of the *bumps* on your body
and all of the *dreams* in your head

you're the *kindness* you cannot keep down
you're the *snort* in your laugh you can't stop
you are all of the *hues* in a rainbow
and quite frankly, you're rather a *lot.*

BENEATH THE SUN

I'm learning . . .
that not everything that shines
is as worthy or as true
as it may seem

I'm learning . . .
that no matter how I toil
someone else will find the faults
I haven't seen

I'm learning . . .
that the women in my life
are more than just my friends
they are my sisters

I'm learning . . .
that holding on too tight
ends with nothing but regret
and nasty blisters

I'm learning . . .
that the body that I chose
is my home
and I am only just a guest

I'm learning . . .
that the perfect people flounder
they falter and they cry
like all the rest

I'm learning . . .
that this life we all receive
is a one-off golden ticket
we have won

I'm learning . . .
that the light we pass along
is the reason we all live
beneath the sun.

If you are the sunshine in someone's cloudy world, I hope you are proud; there is little more valuable than that.

HAPPY

They say happiness is a choice, but I think it's like
day and night. We cannot be happy all of the time,
nor can we be continuously sad. We must let them
interchange, like the sun and the moon. That's the cycle
you see. And yet, they can exist together sometimes
too, a little strangely, a little awkwardly perhaps.
Reminding us life isn't black and white, that emotions
are every colour. And nothing is constant. They say
happiness is a choice, but I think it's peace that we
can choose, peace in the acceptance that life is
everything. And that's okay. A baseline of peace
invites happiness to stay a little longer and lets
sadness come and go, as it must. As it all must.

BACKBONES

A word to the *backbones*
the tireless spines
to the *organisers*
to the reliable
who keep everything aloft
often silently
and without thanks

a word, if you will
to the *always there*
those who lay down
weary
late at night
last to sleep
and first to wake

a word to you
you are
without doubt
needed
but rarely *seen*

perhaps seeing yourself
here
will be a step to saying
thank you

vertebra by vertebra
you are magnificent.

WISH WISELY

All this time, you've been imagining every single thing that could possibly go wrong. Drawing detailed and terrifying pictures in your mind of all the worst-case scenarios. Instead of dreaming, in glorious technicolour, about the wonderful and inspiring things that could go so beautifully *right*. And in doing so, you're providing the universe, the energy that holds us all in place, with a personal transformative plan for your life, a map of what you want and need. A blueprint for joy and peace. You're writing a letter to the stars, each time you imagine something good. Manifesting *magic*. Be careful what you wish for, my friends. Wish wisely.

THE EDGE

Standing at the edge of a new chapter can be scary.
The desire to run back into the pages you know so
well is more than tempting. But you must keep moving.
Chapters end, even the good ones. And if you linger
in the past too long, your story cannot unfold the
way it should. And you might just miss the most
beautiful moments of your life, whilst grieving the
ones gone by. It's scary at the edge my friend, I know.
But just jump. You have so much ahead. And the
good stuff behind, will always be there.

TAUGHT

Perhaps you were never taught
how to love
never shown
the way love works
unconditionally
maybe you had to figure it out
by yourself
the hard way
by giving away parts of you
that were supposed
to stay firmly attached
instead of letting people
come to view your kingdom
you let them make a home
inside your heart
inside your head
and take your bed

perhaps you were never taught
how to love
my friend
and you figured it out
the *hard* way.

THE HEART DOESN'T WANT

The heart wants what it wants, they say,
to explain their devastating chaos, but I don't
blame the heart. I don't think love is a lightning bolt
from above. I don't think love ambushes us from a
happy home and steals us away to another. The heart
needs love, this much is true. But it doesn't want to
crush another heart. It never wants that. And if you fill
your heart with love for yourself, your life, and those
around you, your heart will make great choices. It will
not flee for better views somewhere new, though it may
decide to journey on alone for a while. *The heart wants
what it wants*, they say, but I think the heart always
wants peace. Don't blame hearts for lightning-bolt
devastation and home-wrecking meteors . . .
that's something else entirely.

LIGHTHOUSES AND ROCKS

Some people are lighthouses
they can't help it
they just have so much light within them
that they must use it selflessly
throwing their beams out into the night
with their call of safety and rescue

some people are rocks
they can't help it
they have hardened over the years
grown sharp and edgy
crushing hearts on their craggy points
without even seeing the wreckage
or the survivors drowning before them

some people are lighthouses
and some people are rocks
and you must learn to recognise them
equally
because they are both
as important as the other

one to aim for
and the other to avoid

keep your heart on the lighthouses
and your beady eye on the rocks

you're not going there again.

ROPE LADDER

I have seen a poem **save a life**

I have seen a handful of words
grow legs and arms
run into a burning building
and drag the lifeless out

you may see lines
but I see a *rope ladder* of letters
leading up from rock bottom
to a brighter day

I see a lighthouse
a lifeboat
a helicopter
that roams the mountainside
looking for the lost

I see a message from ancestors
a sign from above
I see *hope*, the thing with wings

you may not consider poetry important
but if you had seen
a poem breathe life
into empty lungs
like I have
you would look anew.

I hope you go easy on yourself
after all you have been through;
everyone deserves kindness at home.

STARDUST

They say human bone
is almost exactly the same makeup
as the breathtaking coral
shimmering gracefully in our oceans

they say stars that erupt
supernova
are responsible
for almost all of the elements
that house our souls

so when you feel small
or insignificant
remember this, sweet one

you really *are* made of stardust
and you are as much a part
of this wonderful world
as the mountains and the seas

the things that blow your mind
the wonders that call you home
do it for good reason
you really *are* made of *stardust*
and you so very much belong.

THE WEARY CHILD WITHIN

There is a tiredness that cannot be slept away.
A weariness that cannot be refreshed with rest.
And when it appears, look straight to your inner child,
my friends. She is the energy, you see. She is the spark
that lights the lamps within, and when your flames are
growing dim, it is she who fires them up once more,
with her youthful, effervescent, boundless supply
of **hope**. If she is weary, that little girl, if she is not
showing up with her light, you need to treat her better.
*She wants freedom, wide spaces to run, she wants
cake, laughter and fun.* She wants to play, my friends,
let her *play*. There is a tiredness that sleep cannot
fight, but laughing, in the moonlight, with your
feet in the sea . . . very much can.

TO THE SEA

When my heart no longer beats
cast me into the ocean, my love

throw my ash atop the water
and watch in reverence
as the moon commands her waves
to embrace every speck of my dust
and wash me into the vast heart
of this magical planet
I was lucky enough to roam

and when you miss me the most
come to the sea, my love

come to the sea
and let Mother Nature remind you
we are all entirely connected
that we may walk this earth
for so many years
but we are part of its bones
forevermore

and as you stand at the water
I will rise up with all my spirit
a breeze lifting the hair from your neck
and breathing life back into your heart

when my heart no longer beats
take me to the sea, my love
take me home.

DO LESS

When you stand at the threshold of a messy
room and you are rendered motionless, unable
to begin, so large is the task facing you, *sit down*.
Do not view the scene as one, but focus in on a single
thing. A shoe, missing its partner perhaps. Complete
the pair, return them to where they live and then sit
down. Think of where you bought that shoe and how
your life unfolded that day and smile for the memory,
no matter how plain. Then focus in on something else
and repeat. It is better to make small steps than to
drown in overwhelm, and your mind is like that too.
When your brain holds too much chaos, *sit down*.
Take one thought at a time, look at it, spin it with
your actual inner voice and not your inner critic,
and place it gently where it should be. When you
want to achieve more, sit down, do *less*.

HOW TO HELP

When bad things are happening
it's common to feel helpless
there is so much wrong
and so little to be done
but *remember*

everything exists in energy
your intentions *matter*

set kindness as your focus
in your little corner of the world
it makes ripples you see
ripples are contagious
they form into waves
and consistent
determined little waves
can move mountains
given time

your kindness
your care
your *hope*
has weight
send it out
send it out

each time you wish a stranger safe
I believe the universe hears.

THE WOMEN BEFORE

It is not just your mother who may walk with you in spirit, it is her mother too, and her mother's mother. And her mother's friends, who loved by choice and not blood. And the women before them. Generations and generations of female energy, watching in admiration as you forge ahead living *better*, feeling *better*, accepting **better**, than they ever did. As they very much hoped you would. So, when you feel low, lonely or unloved, remember them, *feel* them. They are with you, and they burn brightly with their boundless light, in everything you do. You, my friends, are the 'moment in time' of many women gone before, and you will lay pathways, like they did, for those who come up next. What a beautiful, unending legacy.

CHILDREN IN HEAVEN

I spoke to a robin
who visits my tree
I told him I thought
you were waiting for me

he shook his soft head
and much disagreed
the children in heaven
are happy, you see

they know of no fear
they feel no regret
they spend the days wrapped
in a blissful forget

they're loved very much
by your ancestors all
and they run around playing
with sticks and a ball

and the only time
children in heaven seem sad
is when they look down
on the life that they had

and the people they love
feel no longer alive
even though it's not their time
to travel this side

so chin up, said Robin
let no more tears fall
your child is quite free
with their sticks and a ball

and they're in no great rush
to see you just yet
you've life still to live
and more memories to get

and time may pass slowly
here on the ground
but in heaven it's moments
and will quickly come round

so let the world turn
and let everything be
the children in heaven
are *happy*, you see.

If I could hope just one thing for you,
it would be to heal. Your wounds
have been open long enough.

THE SUN

I think it's really vital that you remember the
sun still shines. No matter how thick the cloud, no
matter how many days it's been since you last felt
those rays. They are there. Battling to reach you,
battling to warm the soil and radiate life. And the sun,
she is as keen to get to your weary bones as you are
to feel her. She is on your side. Believe in her, even when
the cloud blocks her out and the world is in darkness.
Knowing she's there is sometimes all you need to come
back. Always, always there. Always, *always* will be.

THEIR LIGHT WILL FIND YOU

We are all full of light
light that no one can actually see
but we *feel* it

we go through life
radiating this light
and shining it on those we love

and when someone we love leaves
it's true
our world really does fall dark
because that light source we couldn't see
but we *felt*
has gone

and it takes a while
it takes time for them to settle
somewhere else
but I promise you that *light*
it shines on us again
from somewhere very different
and we can't see it
but oh we *feel* it

hold on through that dark period
their light will find you
and when it does
it won't ever go dark again.

JUST VISITING

You are not born *to* a land
you are born on it
you are *gifted* access to that soil
but you cannot own a patch of earth
not really

you are a visitor, my friend
we are all visitors
and Mother Nature will often
remind us of this truth

she will rage with her winds
rain with her storm
and swell her mighty oceans to rise
washing away the spoils of human victory
folly and claim

no, she will say, *you do not own this
you are just visiting*

be a good guest
take care of the land you are born on
welcome others to that land
when their ground shakes

you are not born to a land
you are gifted access
do good with the gift

do good with that gift.

IN THE WILD

Much time is ill-spent
striving to be *good*
trying to be someone
the world understood

when most of the world
is doing the same
and it's hard to see who
is playing which game

we hide and we shrink
ourselves into less
in order to fit
we please and say *yes*

and deep down inside
our starved inner child
is wishing and wondering
what's out *in the wild*

tasting the air
for the craved winds of change
a world in which she
may start playing again

and not till too late
do we hear her sad cry
when time is now scarce
and the rivers are dry

don't be this sad tale
of a lost inner child
there's time yet to release
her back to that wild.

FLOWN

Some children flee the nest
and stay *flown*
no return to source
no reunions
or phone calls filled with news
some fledglings fly away
and *stay*
away

and all a mamma bird can do
is hope
and send love
in any way she can
whispering it to the trees
and the butterflies
and the birds that pass each day
praying the words will reach them

waiting
full of love
for the fledglings to *awake*
to the map
that lives in their cells

to *remember*
the way home.

MAGIC

You must believe in the magic. Even on the dreariest
of days, when light is scarce, you must leave space in
your heart for the good stuff to thrive. Let it in. Look
for it. Beautiful moments are everywhere, waiting to
be seen. And each time you see one amongst the mire,
you're reminding every cell in your body that life is
so much more than days in a week and chores on a list.
It is a patchwork kaleidoscope of absolutely everything.
And you are a fascinating, complicated part of that art.

BEFORE YOU SLEEP

Leave guilt on the floor
by your slippers and robe
your worries may nestle there too
let shame and embarrassment
slip through the door
there's no place for such things here with you

let memories of laughter
words aimed to warm
fill up any space in your head
remember the smiles
of the people you love
let those treasures come with you to bed

you did all you could
with the day that you had
you led with that heart full of love
you toil and you care
and that's *always* enough
so release that dark load to above

now rest, close your eyes
let your fears melt away
give in to the slumber you crave
you are giving your all
to this cycle of life
welcome dreams and await a new day.

THE STORY OF YOU

She made a blue book
with her learnings inside
but nobody read it
till after she died

the wrath of her ego
forbade her to share
yet the words she had penned
were droplets of care

then one day
whilst searching for family clues
her granddaughter stumbled
across the blue book

she lost herself reading
the dusty old tome
and with every page turned
felt herself coming home

she rushed to her laptop
and shared with the world
these beautiful stories
the book had unfurled

tales of heartbreak, endurance
of loss, love and gain
a life full of lessons
all free now from shame

the world was entranced
by the chapters they read
the doubt and the worry
had been all in her head

her writing, a *lifeboat*
to those lost at sea
her musings, like torches
the light made them see

so write down your words
in a book, red or blue
there are many who need to read
all you've been through

and as the years pass
and you're gone from their view
your pages will tell them
the story of *you*.

SMALL FIGHTS

Stop allowing yourself to be dragged into small fights.
Leave those petty skirmishes to the small fighters. Let
them argue and debate the news of the day – you have
bigger fish to fry. You have fights that *need* you.
The good fights, the *big* battles. The cages we are
freeing ourselves from, so that those coming after us
can flourish and thrive in our wake. The things that
will *matter*, long after we are gone. Wars that seem too
overwhelming until we join together and show our
strength in undying spirit. Leave the small fights to
the small fighters and save your precious energy for
the causes that enflame and enrage your inner warrior.

THE KARMA THIEF

I think karma is a giant jar of light we store within
our souls. And every time we say or do something
kind, we take light from that jar and give it away.
And karma, being the magical force that it is, will send
that light back to us on days when we need it most.
But that light will be even brighter when it comes
back, because we gave it away in good heart, you see.
Likewise, when we say or do something mean, we also
take light from our jar, light that never comes back.
Light that is disposed of, wasted, sent to the darkness
without ever living its purpose. Light that could have
made this world a better place. And that meanness,
that wasted light, also includes the way you treat
yourself. So if you're wondering why your karma does
not reflect your kind heart, check your inner critic.
She may have been quite busy, stealing light.

YOUIER

Imagine if the moon refused to shine
because the sun was *shinier*

if streams ceased to flow
because the rivers were *flowier*

if snow didn't dare to fall
because rain was *fallier*

if planets did not glow
because stars were *glowier*

what a world it would be
if nature compared

if flowers didn't flower
because their neighbours were *flowerier*

you, my friend, must stop all that folly

no one can be more you
you are **youier**.

THE PEACE THEY NOW FEEL

They're not angry
those you lost
wherever they may be
they're not bitter
or traumatised
they're not hoarding regret
nor are they interested
in retribution or revenge

they are at peace

and if you believe
that they flow alongside us
in essence
then you can be certain
they would wish only for us
to feel that peace
they now know
and their love

so, if you are feeling any
of the painful emotions above
in honour of your loved ones passed over
please find a way to release it to the heavens

they will take it for you and let it go

they're not angry
those you lost
they are at peace
let them share with you
the peace they now feel
it was hard won.

I will come in spirit to dry your tears,
my love, but I hope you will gift me your laughter
often too – my favourite sound of all.

COME SIT WITH ME

If you are *too much*
too emotional
too sensitive
too loud
too honest
too deep
too loving

come sit with me

and we can pool our too-muchness
and send it up to the moon
to scatter amongst the stars
let our too-muchness
find solace in their brilliance
expand a million times more
and shower the world
with that light
of *too much person*
for one person

if you are too much
come sit with me, my friend

I like *too much*
you can be too much
and more
with me.

IT'S YOUR WEIRD I WANT

Let me tell you a little secret: the best people I ever met were weird. So deliciously not-normal that I delighted with every layer peeled back of their shimmering, onion-like soul. So weird, that each time I saw them I waited with bated breath to behold which pearls of wisdom they would bestow upon me, what treasures they would reveal, from their pirate chest of *life* and what wisdom they would impart from their hair-raising, life-seeking adventures. I revel in the weird and the wonderful, the new and the unique, the free and the quirky. So do not wear your normal for me, dear heart, it's your weird I came to see. It's your weird I very much want to meet.

WILD HOPE

You cannot tame hope
or make it care for fact
nor can you shame hope
or talk to it of lack

hope will listen not
to your worries or your fears
it listens only to your soul
to your inner child's tears

hope will rise in spite of pain
against the storm and quake
hope will walk through burning flame
quench fire in its wake

you cannot tame hope
or make it bend the knee
it grows wild and all around
hope costs nothing
hope is free

simply reach within your soul
to the place where instincts meet
and there you'll find this hope
growing **wild**
and growing *deep*.

LOVE CAME FIRST

You don't move on after loss, but you must move
with. You must shake hands with grief, welcome
her in, for she lives with you now. Pull her a chair
at the table and offer her comfort. She is not the
monster you first thought her to be. She is *love*.
And she will walk with you now, *stay* with you now,
peacefully. If you let her. And on the days when your
anger is high, remember why she came, remember
who she represents. *Remember*. Grief came to you,
my friend, because love came first. *Love came first.*

THE *WITHOUT YOU*

After all the *firsts* without you
which came in like wrecking balls
I exhausted my memories of our *lasts* too
and felt as though a new grief had appeared
no more of these milestones left
so what now?

I thought the *now* must be without you
until I felt your smile
felt it *warm* my skin
as your song played out on the radio

and then that proud moment
the one I thought I'd never see
you were there at my shoulder
I *knew* it

when hard decisions arise
somehow your advice appears
as though you planted it inside me

so here I am
greeting the robins you send me
counting the feathers you drop
and the rainbows you draw
realising
there is a new chapter of us
we are not *done*

it's different
but it is something
and until we meet again
I will make it enough.

SHOW YOUR CARDS

I know it's hard
to let people see the real you
like showing your whole hand of cards
at the start of a game
you won't win

but life isn't a card game
and this world needs your authentic self

there are too many copies out there
keeping things inside
going through the motions
and at least one of those people
is searching with desperate eyes
for someone to emulate
someone who is out there
being themselves
despite life and its losses

if you show yourself to them
they will blossom
and you will too
and so it will go on

you may never win the card game, my friend
but if you are the reason
someone blossoms

you're a winner
be brave

the world needs it.

GOOD

Most people are good. Most people kiss their
pets goodbye and read *just one more* bedtime story
to their children. Most people visit their grandparents
even when they have no time and stop by to check
on quiet friends after a long day. Most people return
their shopping trolleys, despite being already late,
and let someone with only one item jump to the front
of a queue. Most people give money when money is
scarce and most people worry about people they don't
even know, day in and day out. When the world
seems bad, remember, most people are **good**.

THAT THING YOU DO

That thing you do, that thing you're just *good* at. The thing that has always drawn you in, from childhood. That thing that has brought you *something* the rest of the world can't see. You should do that, much more often. It doesn't matter if it makes you money, or if anyone else thinks it's worthwhile. It's your *thing*. And every time another adult does their thing *again*, something in the universe shifts. It's like pieces of a puzzle that was never supposed to make sense, but was always supposed to just *be*. You must do your thing again, my friend. It matters.

Hope lives deep; it's the empty space within your bones that makes them so intricately strong. And when they break, strap them up; hope will mend itself.

WILDLINGS

This goes out to the mamas
raising the wild ones
the *not to be tamed*
the rare
the reckless
and the *precious*

you are shaping stardust
into human form
minding moonlight
till it's ready to instruct the tides
and light the nights

do not expect the world to see
your diamond in the rough
sparkle
not yet
they *cannot*

but one day
they will be unable
to take their eyes away
from its shine

to the mamas of the wild ones
you are star gatherers
moon catchers
and dream shapers

and you are exhausted

but shaping starlight
into human form
was always going to be tough
and you are.

GREAT FRIENDS

They say great friends are like stars
you don't always see them
but they're always there
I have definitely found this to be true

some days there is little time
to check my stars are doing okay
and yet my brain – no, wait, my *heart*
sends out that message somehow

I like to think the sentiment
gets to where it was going
as though the message of
I am here if you need me
and *I think of you often*
rises up through the atmosphere
bounces off each star
until it finds the one
I aimed it at
you

if great friends are like stars
I am playing a cosmic pin-ball game
of beautiful, grateful thoughts with mine
and occasionally I even pick up the phone
but I am always, always there
always, *always* will be.

YESTERDAY'S RUBBISH

As sure as night follows day, pain will follow joy. As sure as summer follows spring, good times will be met by bad. We each have our share. And all you need to know is that nothing lasts. Bad times, as is their nature, feel like the end. They convince you you won't survive another moment. But you will. And you do, and you *have,* a million times before. And it is perfectly *okay* to lament your misfortune, to beat your breast and scream, *why me.* We all do it. But once that anger, that rage, has had its moment, be free of it. Put it down, like a plate straight from the oven. You will need your hands free, you see. To welcome the *new,* when the storm is over. Because all storms run out of rain. All skies clear eventually. And you won't get your share of the good stuff if you're carrying yesterday's rubbish. See each new dawn as a chance to be free of the past. New page, clean slate, hands free.

TINY FINGERS

I can still feel tiny fingers
wrapped around my thumb
and the brush of little lashes
on my cheeks
it seems but scarce a moment
since I held you in one arm
and rocked you back and forth
to help you sleep

I remember wobbly steps
as you fought to stand up tall
the joy of each success
bright in your eyes
I remember all the monsters
I banished from your bed
how I'd be the one to soothe you
when you cried

I'm still that mum who worries
if your life is going well
if I raised you with enough
to have it all
but if be truth be told, my darling
it's just love I want for you
and the wonder that you had
when you were small

and you fly so very high
higher than I ever did
and that, my love, is just
how this should play
in my mind you'll always be
tiny fingers round my thumb
and I'll rock you there
until my dying day.

YOUR SKY

I never truly noticed
how beautiful the sky is
until I started searching it

for you

I never really appreciated
how sunlight
bounces off the clouds sometimes
creating a glimmeringly spectacular
show of light

but now it feels as though
you are putting that show on
just for me

I sit in the front row
and consume your blinding light
to feel your spirit near
with all my earthly might

I never truly noticed
how wondrously uplifting
the sky is, my love

until I started searching it for you

until it became *your sky*

and I search your sky daily
and always will.

LIFE AND SOUL

Everyone knows a *life and soul*
who isn't here anymore
everyone knows a *character*
with that smile so very bright
who left us way too soon

it is often said, by so many of us
they didn't seem sad at all

and so let us pay more attention
to the *life and souls*
the characters
the bright-smilers and never-weepers

let us no longer accept their distractions
their re-routing of your questions
with jokes and sparkle
let us ask them twice
and once more for luck
how are you, really?

for those life and souls are often that way
because they understand
what deep pain can do to a heart

so they spread light with intention
whilst covering their own darkness

let us vow to protect
those diamonds in the rough
you and I
they are just too precious to lose.

TAKE THEIR BREATH

When grief is squeezing
air from your lungs
take a breath
deeply
for your self
and one for those
who can no longer

take their breath too

fill your lungs
cell by cell
with precious life-giving air
and feel it feed your brain
your heart
your body

feel the life

when the grief is squeezing you out
breathe in

and take another
miraculous breath
for those who can no longer

it will keep you alive

and they will feel it.

If hope were a person she would have mud on her knees, dirt under her nails and determination on her tear-stained but smiling face.

SISTERHOOD

When I have been stuck, *cocooned* in this life, it was
women who came to free me. Women who reminded me
what I am made of and what I am *becoming*. Women,
who broke my shell, reached for my hands and pulled
me out. Not just to fly again, but to fly higher than ever
before. There is much beauty, much ancient history,
in that intuitive network of strength, support and silent
sisterhood. Treasure it, as you would a very special gift,
because that's what it is, my sisters, *that is what it is*.

UNSPOKEN LOVE

What happens to the compliments
that live their life unsaid
all the lovely thoughts you keep
so silent in your head?

each of those expressions
might have warmed a frozen heart
or planted seeds within a mind
so something new could start

and what of those *I love yous*
that rushed up to your throat
yet lingered there unvoiced
the *love you never spoke*

your mind is full enough
of words you wish you'd said
don't add to that the love you felt
but made small talk instead

words, you see, hold power
they carry what they *are*
they take their message with them
and travel oh so far

so when they tiptoe lightly
on your tongue next time you chat
speak those words and let them fly
to find somebody's heart.

LIFE AND DEATH

Nothing will jolt you alive with quite as much passion as realising we will all die one day. There is no better way to embrace life than to contemplate death. It is not morbid, to let your mind consider what is ahead of each and every one of us. It is the opposite. It is a life-affirming, soul-shaking, head-wobbling, stop-and-smell-the-roses injection of what truly matters. It will transport you, quickly, into the moment. And you will look around with a clearer vision, heightened senses and a love for the ordinary. Are you there? Welcome. Now let's begin the act of living. We have no time to lose.

UNTOLD GLORY

If the world lost its infrastructure overnight
and we all came together to rebuild
who would you become?

a planner or a carer
perhaps you'd be a forager
or a healer
you may rise to the fore as a leader
take to the fields as a farmer
or work with your hands to build new
you might be the storyteller
the *music* or the *art*

perhaps if life was more simple
we would not struggle to recognise our gifts
it would be obvious
natural
we would simply pick up tools
and do what we *know*
intrinsically
the things our soul just gets

if you are feeling *less than*
remember
we are not here to explode
in a giant ball of mesmerising light
drowning the world with our brilliance

we are simply here to live

and there is much skill
much *untold glory*
in the things you do so beautifully
every day.

LET YOUR WOUNDS CLOSE

Let your wounds close. Do not pick at them
as they heal. There is much valour in this act of
stitching up raw flesh, soul and heart, much science,
much magic, much *closure*. Let them. Do not press
them to make them hurt, do not scratch them when
they itch. Let your wounds heal, my love. It is okay,
it is commendable in fact, to be half skin, half scars in
this life. But you have no time to be walking around
unhealed, with open, festering wounds. Let them close.
Let them seal. Let them *heal*. One day, not so far away,
you will trace your finger around the silvery shine of
their new surface, and remember what you overcame.

WHAT YOU HAVE

Someone somewhere
would love your home
would covet your car
and the clothes you disown

someone somewhere
adores your nose
and the way your hair
so wildly grows

to someone somewhere
your life's but a dream
a beautiful tale
of which you're the queen

someone right now
is wishing to be
as tall as you
and as short as me

yet here we are
thinking the same
wishing we had
other things in this game

staring with envy
at what we have not
instead of being grateful
for all that we've got.

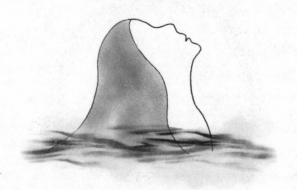

HANG ON

There are times, and there will be more, when answers
are simply not within reach. And that's okay. They're
not supposed to be. I think these times are for practising
hope. For *believing*. For surrendering to the *knowing*
that a plan will emerge. That a path will appear.
That a way *through* will simply transpire, given space
and time to form. That life will move on, placing you
exactly where you are supposed to be. Just as the ocean
will always deliver that message in a bottle to a beach.
Sometimes, we are not supposed to *know*. We are
supposed to *believe*. To *hope*. To hang on.
Just hang on, my friends, *hang on*.

DO NOT SLEEP WITH WORRY

Do not sleep with worry
worry is no good in bed
he will interrupt your slumber
spinning dramas like a web

he will plant seeds in your garden
they will strangle all you've grown
pulling roots up from your flowerbeds
to make room there for his own

he will take your precious memories
and paint them murky grey
he will meet your inner child
and send her cowering on her way

do not let him in your bed, love
crack the window, shoo him out
throw his friends out there to join him
fear, perfection and self-doubt

now quickly, close the window
come back and snuggle down
and check that only good thoughts
are allowed to stick around

let hope and joy come by
they are soothing, wise and true
add acceptance to the mix
then let peace wash over you

no do not sleep with worry
worry is no good in bed
you have stress enough in life
to let that monster in your head.

THIS ROCK

We exist on a 4.5-billion-year-old rock
floating in an unfathomable expanse
of *nothingness*
you and I
we are magnetically held in place
by an invisible force
along with 8 billion other people

every single thing that exists on this rock
is without doubt a work of art
so intricately crafted
we will never truly discover
the scope of wonder within

we are made of the same elements
as everything that naturally surrounds us
just shaken up differently
and oh so *magnificently*

look at us, my friends
we are *breathtaking*
our breath alone
the power in that act
is *breathtaking*

everything you are doing right now
reading, feeling, understanding
is *fascinatingly* complex
and yet we spend our days *worrying*
about things
that are of no significance at all
big-picture

walk around your world today
with awe in your eyes
and really see what you are *living*

every aspect of this life
is nothing short of astonishing
and this rock we are clinging to with ease
is *astounding*

eyes open, reach out, breathe deep

take it all in

this rock, our *home*
will know each of us
for only a heartbeat in its timeline

leave only love
live with only gratitude
look with only wonder.

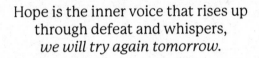

Hope is the inner voice that rises up
through defeat and whispers,
we will try again tomorrow.

I REALLY DO

I hope life brings you moments of utter joy.
When nothing but the fear of it ending can interfere
with your happiness. And I hope you pick that fear up
and throw it on your shoulders like a backpack.
You can't outrun it, but you can definitely go ahead
with it anyway, and you *must*. I hope life brings you
moments of perfect peace too, when the stillness of this
vast planet reveals itself to you and whispers, *This is
where the beauty lies*. I hope you see colours every day,
and hear music when no music is playing. I hope there
are days when the sun is warm, the breeze is on your
skin and the laughter is loud. I hope you *live* sometimes,
and connect to the source of all that matters.
And I hope today is that day. I really do.

AFTERWORD

Thank you for reading this book. I *hope* you found *hope* here. And I *hope* most of all that you found a safe place for you to just *be*, as you are, flaws and all. Do come and join me on social media if you haven't already. It's a daily reminder, you see, a reminder to just live, messily, imperfectly and beautifully. Come sit with me; whether healed, grieving, broken, radiant, raw or at peace. I will be delighted to have you, whichever way you arrive.

ACKNOWLEDGEMENTS

There are so many people I would like to thank,
but I'm going to start with those who follow me on
social media. This may sound cheesy, but I adore you
all! These fiercely supportive women (you know who
you are) who share their trials and tribulations with
me daily and allow me an insight into their worlds.
This act allows me to serve others better with my
writing and for that, and the emotional connection,
I am so very grateful and I value you wildly! Thank you
for being on this road with me – I never feel lonely.

I would also love to thank my friends Jennie and Lynn
for their constant ears, shoulders and hearts, and my
sister Nanette who has taken over my Gran's position
as chief cheerleader and number-one fan. My mum
Elizabeth, who never stops growing, evolving and
inspiring me with her journey and my dad Derek,
who loves to joke that he is never thanked (ha!) –
you are always full of advice I did not know I needed,
I love you! Further acknowledgement (in writing because
I know you will be delighted) to my Niomi and Emma.
You show me that time and distance mean nothing
in the face of true friendship.

A huge thanks to my editor Susanna too.
You have brought calm, knowing and structure when
I needed it most and working with you feels like home.
Thanks to all my team at B&W Publishing and
Bonnier Books – coming to London to get the
big-city treatment is such a joy!

I would also love to acknowledge the wonderful Lisa Snowdon and Davina McCall who have both given me words of encouragement to display proudly with my book. You are both so busy and yet so generous with your time. The work you are doing for women in their menopausal years is shining desperately needed light into dark places and is bringing out those who may otherwise have been lost along the way.

A huge thank you to my husband Robert. Thank you for being there no matter what, and for striving to be better every day. You are amazing, and I am beyond lucky to have you and our boys.

Thank you as well to my dogs, Dave and Brian, who keep me inspired and at peace during my working day with their cuddles and unconditional love.

Lastly, I cannot leave this place without remembering Dame Deborah James whose 'Rebellious Hope' deeply inspired me, and so many others. Oh Deborah, you live on, in so many ways! We carry you with us, thank you.

ABOUT THE AUTHOR

Donna Ashworth is a *Sunday Times* bestselling poet
who lives in the hills of Scotland with her husband,
two sons, and Brian and Dave (the dogs).

Donna started her social media accounts in 2018
in a bid to create a 'safe' social space for women
to come together and connect, but her love of all
things wordy quickly became the focus, and a
past love for poetry was reignited. Seven books and
over one million followers later, Donna is delighted
daily with her mission to shower the world with
words and bring poetry back into focus.

'My head is a constant fizz of emotions, poetry
and prose, so it's a delight to be able to release those
bath-bombs into the world and watch the bubbles travel.
I believe the right words, at the right time, hold so
much power, can bring huge comfort and are
vital in these troubled times.'

Facebook @DonnaAshworth
Instagram @DonnaAshworthWords
TikTok @DonnaAshworthWordy
Twitter @donna_ashworth

If you've enjoyed *Wild Hope* you may also love:

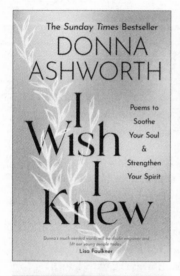

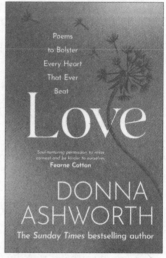

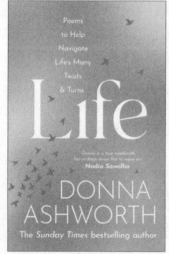

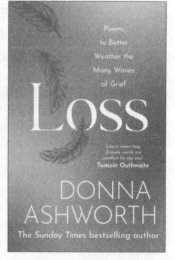

Mango Publishing, established in 2014, publishes an eclectic list of books by diverse authors—both new and established voices—on topics ranging from business, personal growth, women's empowerment, LGBTQ studies, health, and spirituality to history, popular culture, time management, decluttering, lifestyle, mental wellness, aging, and sustainable living. We were named 2019 and 2020's #1 fastest growing independent publisher by Publishers Weekly. Our success is driven by our main goal, which is to publish high-quality books that will entertain readers as well as make a positive difference in their lives.

Our readers are our most important resource; we value your input, suggestions, and ideas. We'd love to hear from you—after all, we are publishing books for you!

Please stay in touch with us and follow us at:

Facebook: Mango Publishing

Twitter: @MangoPublishing

Instagram: @MangoPublishing

LinkedIn: Mango Publishing

Pinterest: Mango Publishing

Newsletter: mangopublishinggroup.com/newsletter

Join us on Mango's journey to reinvent publishing, one book at a time.